ARTICULATING STRENGTHS TOGETHER (AST)

AN INTERACTIVE PROCESS
TO ENHANCE POSITIVITY

Jerald R. Forster, PhD

D1401217

CONTENTS

PART 1: WHAT IS THE *AST* AND WHY SHOULD YOU USE IT?

PART 2: HOW DO YOU FACILITATE THE AST PROCESS?

FOREWORD

Bernard Haldane developed the key ideas underlying the process described in this book during a period of sixty years, from 1942 to 2002. It was 1987 when Bernard and I started the Dependable Strengths Project at the University of Washington where I had been a faculty member in the College of Education since 1966. Before we began our collaboration, I had been involved in research and development activities designed to help participants articulate their goals and the attributes that they wanted in their future jobs. My primary contribution to Bernard's work was to help him conceptualize his practices of facilitating personal exploration and clarification, as articulation processes. He liked my suggestion that he call his most recently developed version, the *Dependable Strengths Articulation Process (DSAP)*. Of all the activities he devised for the DSAP, his idea of having four participants talk about their good experiences together, as they helped each other articulate their strengths, was my favorite. We eventually came to call this part of the process "the quad activity."

While the quad activity always generated lots of good insights and good feelings, it was somewhat complicated and required trained facilitators for guidance. I always saw this requirement for a trained facilitator as a hurdle for broad implementation. That is why I have been determined to create a simplified process that enables participants to experience the basic process in the most efficient and least cumbersome format. So, I went back to some of the skills I had developed before meeting Bernard, and developed an articulation process that could be self-guided in a three-hour period.

JRF

ACKNOWLEDGMENTS

In addition to the crucial contribution of Bernard Haldane, Jean Haldane and Allen Boivin-Brown must be acknowledged for their work in helping to develop the quad activity to its current level of usefulness.

Other members of the Executive Committee making up the non-profit organization, the Center for Dependable Strengths (CDS), have made contributions to the success of the DSAP, and therefore the writing of this book. Eight of the Executive Committee members are shown in the photographs on the front and back covers of this book. On the front cover, from left to right, are Katie Hearn Zang, Sharon Allen-Felton, Jerald Forster, and Allen Boivin-Brown. On the back cover are Sheri Adams, Patrice Tabor, Dean Summers, and Vic Snyder. Susan Terry, Wendy Davis, and Bob Pack are three other members of the CDS Executive Committee, who were not available when the photographs were taken.

Kate Forster, my talented and supportive partner in life, took the cover photographs for this book. More importantly, Kate is one of the best editors that an author could hope for. In addition, Kate's daughter, Jennifer Rose, a professional editor in New York City, provided very insightful editorial assistance.

I feel very fortunate that the people mentioned above have been a part of my life and the writing of this book.

JRF

PART 1:

WHAT IS THE *AST* AND WHY SHOULD YOU USE IT?

Introduction

The purpose of the AST is to guide you and three others through a series of activities that will give each participant a list of his or her most valued personal strengths. This process was adapted from the longer Dependable Strengths Articulation Process (DSAP), which was developed by Bernard Haldane during the second half of the 20th Century.[1] The DSAP has been packaged with another process developed by Bernard Haldane,[2] the Job Magnet system, to form an 18-hour workshop that helps participants articulate their Dependable Strengths® and then write a Dependable Strengths Report. The resulting report is useful as the participants seek employment that fits their unique pattern of strengths.

The interactive process offered in the AST follows a carefully developed sequence of activities that can be completed in about three hours. The AST process guides four participants through activities wherein they recall very positive experiences and then share these experiences with other members of the four-person group, which will hereafter be called a *quad*. Participants take turns talking about their experiences, while others in the quad list the names of possible strengths that were demonstrated by the experiences being described. Then, each participant considers the suggested strengths and other strengths listed in the workbook, eventually prioritizing the ones that seem most relevant. These prioritized strengths are then described on a poster, along with examples of prior events when those strengths were demonstrated.

The descriptions on each participant's poster are the products of the process. However, these results should only be considered as a current draft of an evolving articulation process likely to continue during each participant's lifetime. Your self-identity is always changing, hopefully in an evolving spiral that builds on your awareness of your most significant strengths. There is a great deal of evidence that you will benefit from articulating your strengths and becoming more strengths-focused in your awareness of yourself and those with whom you interact.[3]

What are *Strengths,* and what is *Articulation?*

Strengths are positive qualities associated with being strong and capable. Strengths enable you to resist threats to your wellbeing and to endure onslaughts that might leave you vulnerable. When you focus on strengths you are focusing on qualities that enable you and others to thrive. When you focus on strengths you are automatically looking for positive ways of characterizing whatever is the focus of your attention, be it yourself, other people, or even objects such as buildings or vehicles. When you are looking for and recognizing strengths, your perspective is positive, the essence of positive psychology, and the mark of a healthy, thriving person.

You are *articulate* when you are able to communicate complex ideas and feelings with clarity and accuracy. Articulation is a process of expressing oneself readily, clearly and effectively. If you are articulating your strengths, you are identifying and communicating your most positive qualities. The qualities that you are trying to articulate are complex and changing. You may use many levels of abstraction when describing these strengths, which means that the process of articulating your strengths can be challenging and sometimes confusing. There is no final or absolute language for describing personal strengths. There are no "just right" descriptions that you can finally articulate in order to capture the essence of who you are. The process of articulating your strengths is a continuing, lifetime endeavor that can always be improved so as to capture your changing identity as you grow and develop.

Why should you articulate your strengths?

Most people are striving to have the best life they can. I assume that you have tried to live your life in a way that enables you to be happy and successful, feeling good about your accomplishments. This AST process was designed to help you realize as many of those outcomes as possible. Theorists, researchers, and practitioners identifying with the *positive psychology movement*[4] have developed a growing body of theory, research and practice that provides a solid framework for, and scientific evidence of the benefits of, participating in activities like those suggested in this process[5]. Practitioners in fields of psychology, education, organizational development and other social sciences have recognized the value of focusing on the positive.[6] A large number of studies have shown that positive emotions are beneficial.[7] Positive emotions accompany thoughts about the strengths you might be using in the present, and they also occur when you feel grateful for past experiences that were satisfying to you. You also feel positive emotions when you look forward to positive experiences that you expect to have in the future. In other words, your attitudes and feelings of gratitude,[8] optimism[9] and hope[10] are also strengths. All of these strengths are correlated with mental, emotional and physical health, as well as success in the workplace and in schools[11], when participants in relationships and organizations focus their attention on each other's strengths, they experience positive emotions, which result in better morale and productivity.[12] Research by the Gallup Organization demonstrates that people who have an opportunity to use their strengths are motivated to work harder, and the productivity of their organization increases as a result.[13] Similarly, personal relationships that are strengths-focused are more beneficial to the participants than are those focused on weaknesses and negativity.[14] Marriages and other relationships in families last longer and result in greater personal development when focus on strengths is increased.[15] This newfound emphasis on strengths has been called a *strengths revolution*.[16]

Why should you articulate your strengths together?

It is easy to say why you should articulate your strengths, but why should you include others in the process of articulating your strengths? The reason is that your self-identity is mainly a function of your interactions with others. We all use other people as mirrors, to reflect views of ourselves. Humans are relational beings who construct their identities from feedback and observations coming from others. You are likely to consider the reactions and the opinions of others if you think they know something about you and if you believe they are capable of making accurate or valid observations.

Also, you are likely to take some of your strengths for granted because they come so easily for you. You are so used to these particular strengths that you are hardly aware of them. When others hear you describe something you did very well, they may immediately see the strengths that were involved, while you may have not noticed them, or possibly discounted them because they were so easy.

Another benefit of having others recognize your strengths is that you may have not acknowledged some of your strengths because you felt like others would think you were bragging. When others identify these positive qualities first, you can then modestly agree that maybe you do have those particular strengths.

In other words, the observations or opinions of others are likely to be quite useful to you. If you are like most people, you are always looking for information that will help you understand yourself a little better. You are likely to appreciate that information if it comes from others. This will especially be the case if the information is positive and judged to be valid.

The number of people who are giving you the information may well be a factor influencing your judgments about the validity and reliability of the information you are getting. This is why it is useful to have more than one person giving you information about yourself. When at least three people, who have heard your stories of positive experiences, give you feedback that is coherent and repetitive, you are likely to pay more attention to the information than if you heard it from one or two. It would be even better to have more people give you feedback, if there were time. However, there is often a tradeoff between the time available and the value of variety and repetition in feedback. Four people sharing their experiences and receiving feedback from others appears to be an optimal number.

Although the reactions you get from others are more powerful if they come from several people, reactions from one can also be very meaningful and useful. Because of this, you can also use the AST process with one, two or three people. While it is less likely to be as powerful, the basic interactive process can be used with fewer than four people.

Why should you also attend a Dependable Strengths® workshop?

After articulating your strengths using the AST process, you would benefit from articulating your *Dependable* Strengths by participating in workshops that include the full Dependable Strengths Articulation Process (DSAP). This is especially true if you are currently in the job market, or looking forward to a change of career. While the AST process will help you articulate strengths that may well be Dependable Strengths, it may be insufficient for getting a job that uses your strengths. The depth of the DSAP experience adds to and reinforces your understanding of what you have to offer a potential employer. Led by a trained facilitator, the DSAP goes beyond the scope of the AST because it is usually packaged with the Job Magnet system that is offered by the Center for Dependable Strengths (CDS) or CDS-trained facilitators. In this 18-hour workshop, you will develop a Strengths Report that you can then use to gain referrals from helpful people who look at your Report and suggest possible referrals. If you follow the guidelines offered during this Job Magnet process, you are more likely to locate people and organizations that would value your particular pattern of strengths. These people might help you gain employment where you could use your strengths in an optimal way.

If you want to learn more about the DSAP and the workshops designed to help you find employment where you can use your Dependable Strengths, access the CDS website at www.dependablestrengths.org.

What is the value of becoming more strengths-focused?

One of the goals of the exploration process guided by the AST process is to become more *strengths focused*. To be more strengths-focused, you would need to pay more attention to your own strengths and to the strengths of people with whom you interact. If you did this, you would, by definition, become more positive in your perceptions. When you focus on your own strengths and the strengths of others, you are focusing on positive qualities. If you want to read about the potential value of focusing on positive qualities, read Barbara Fredrickson's 2009 book, *Positivity*. In this research-based book, Fredrickson builds a strong case for the value of a positive perspective and the positive emotions that can be generated by a positive perspective. In addition to Fredrickson's book, there are a large number of books and articles that make this same case. There is an extensive body of research and literature supporting the idea that you and others will benefit if you can develop a more positive perspective that is strengths-focused.

How could you create a strengths-focused community?

A strengths-focused community is simply a group of people who agree that they will intentionally pay more attention to strengths when they interact with each other. If you are still in the initial stage of selecting three other people to complete the activities of this AST process, you could talk to the prospective participants about the possibility of creating a strengths-based community among the four of you. After all, a community can be of any size. It can be four people who agree to interact with a common purpose, such as supporting each other to develop more positive perspectives about the people in their lives.

While the four of you could start with the intention of developing strengths-focused relationships and a strengths-focused community, it is also possible to decide to do this after you have completed the AST process. Actually, this might be the more likely scenario, in that the feelings resulting from the AST process are likely to create a desire for even more interactions with the people associated with the stimulation of these positive feelings. These desires are likely to stimulate additional possibilities for strengths-based relationships and communities. People like to be with people with whom they feel good. That is usually what happens when you participate in the AST process.

The AST process could also be used in your work setting. Can you imagine trying this process with three other people with whom you work on a daily basis? Could the people at your work place agree to meet with others in quads with the intention of making the entire organization a community that focuses on strengths? If you wanted to use it more selectively at your work place, you could use it to develop strengths-focused teams. To implement this approach, you might locate informal or formal teams that consist of 3 to 5 co-workers who work closely on common projects. These team members would benefit greatly from knowing more about each other's strengths, so that team responsibilities might be modified, allowing each team member to better use his or her strengths.

Or, could you organize a number of quads within your religious community and create a congregation that focuses on strengths?

The idea could even spread to sports teams, where team members would come to value the individual strengths of other team members.

You could use this process to make your social life more enriched, by using it as:

- a format for what used to be called, a "double date," when two couples get together to do the AST as a foursome; or as

- an activity at a singles organization, when participants learn more about each other by exploring their strengths together; or as

- a social activity at a college dorm, when students team up with other students to articulate their strengths; or as

- an opportunity to deepen supportive relationships in healing communities such as AA and others; or as

- a means of offering support to a family member, friend, or other community member who is engaged in a job search, or just feeling down.

Are there objective instruments that might extend your strengths articulation beyond the AST?

The AST is a subjective process, not an objective instrument. The activities of the AST process were designed to help you articulate your own subjective perceptions of your strengths. These perceptions are very important because they represent the way you currently see yourself in terms of positive qualities. Your self-identity is likely to be strongly influenced by your subjective understanding of the qualities you attribute to yourself. These subjective, self-perceived attributions have been influenced a great deal by the perceptions of people with whom you have had considerable interaction, such as your family members, your friends and others with whom you have interacted a good deal.

In addition to these sources of information about your personal strengths, you could also benefit from the results of objective instruments or inventories of your strengths. There are several inventories or objective instruments that have been developed to help you learn about your possible strengths. Two of the most accessible objective approaches are: (1) *Strengths Finder (2.0)* & (2) The *VIA-IS (Institute Survey)* or the *VIA Survey of Character*. If you are interested, you might access these surveys, respond to them and then study the results.

Information about The *Strengths Finder 2.0* assessment instrument can be obtained online at: <https://www.strengthsfinder.com/>. The most common method of obtaining results about your own strengths is to purchase the book[17], *Strengths Finder 2.0* by Tom Rath. This book costs about $12 and it provides an access code that will provide a 20-page report about the top five themes of your strengths.

Information about the *VIA Survey of Character*[18] can be obtained online at: <http://www.viastrengths.org/>. You can take the *VIA Survey* by registering and then taking a free online survey that identifies your unique profile of character strengths. Your profile will show which five character strengths, of the 24 identified by this instrument, best represent the way you described yourself when responding to the questions. The 24 character strengths identified by the *VIA Survey* are described by the authors of the instrument as universal characteristics that define what's best about people.

A third online strengths assessment tool[19], the *Realise2*, was published in 2009. The Center of Applied Positive Psychology offers this instrument to the public and it can be accessed through <http://www.cappeu.org/realise2.htm>. The cost of *Realise2* is 15 Sterling Pounds (including VAT), paid for by using the online *Paypal* system through a secure server. You get back a comprehensive

Profile Report showing your *Realised Strengths, Unrealised Strengths, Learned Behaviours* and *Weaknesses.*

Each of these online inventories or surveys takes about 30 minutes to complete. The results are sent to your e-mail address.

If you study the results from these three survey instruments, you are likely to increase your vocabulary for describing your strengths, in addition to seeing patterns as to how your strengths might be organized. This new knowledge can be used to elaborate your own ways of describing your strengths. Keep in mind, however, that new vocabulary words will be of limited value unless you can identify personal experiences that give meaning to these words. We cannot stress the value of personal experience enough. That is why the personal experiences called *Good Experiences* are so valuable in the process that you will do in your quads. The strengths identified in that process are tied to real-life experiences, so they have personal meanings. The words elicited by objective surveys are less likely to be tied to personal experiences you have had. Strengths words that can be anchored to real experiences are likely to have more personal meanings that lead to a more strengths-based self-identity. This is not to say that strength words identified from objective surveys and inventories cannot have personal meaning, it only means that you have to work harder to relate these words to your personal experiences. The words for strengths identified by these objective inventories need to be defined for you, so you can try to relate them to words that you regularly use to describe experiences you can remember.

* * *

REFERENCES AND NOTES FOR PART I

1. Forster, J. R. (2003). "Bernard Haldane was ahead of his time," in a special issue: The Influence of Bernard Haldane. (Edited by K. Duttro). *Career Planning & Adult Development Journal*, 19:3, 28-38.

2. Haldane, B. (1996). *Career satisfaction and success: A guide to job and personal freedom.* Indianapolis, IN: JIST Works, Inc.

3. Forster, J. R. (2005). *A summary of selected positive psychology literature supporting strengths articulation,* A paper presented at the 16th International Congress of the Psychology of Personal Constructs. Columbus, OH. July 19, 2005. (Internet access address: <www.dependablestrengths.org>)

4. Seligman, M. E. (2002). *Authentic happiness.* NY: Free Press.

5. Two books published in 2008 describe numerous studies that support interventions leading to increased focus on positivity and happiness. One book is: Lyubomirsky, S. (2008), *The how of happiness.* NY: Penguin Press; The other book is: Diener, E., & Biswas-Diener, R. (2008), *Happiness: Unlocking the mysteries of psychological wealth.* Oxford: Blackwell Publications; The most comprehensive body of evidence that positive psychology interventions significantly enhance well-being and decrease depressive symptoms can be found in the following article: Sin, N.L. & Lyuboirsky, S. (2009). "Enhancing well-being and alleviating depressive symptoms with positive psychology interventions: A practice-friendly meta-analysis." *Journal of Clinical Psychology: In Session.* 65(5), 487-487.

6. Carr, A. (2004). *Positive psychology: The science of happiness and human strengths.* NY: Brunner-Routledge.

7. Fredrickson, B. (2009). *Positivity.* NY: Crown Publishers.

8. Emmons, R. A. (2007). *THANKS! How the new science of gratitude can make you happier.* NY: Houghton Mifflin.

9. Scheier, M. F., Carver, C. S., & Bridges, M. W. (2001). Optimism, pessimism, and psychological well-being. In E. C. Chang (Ed.), *Optimism and pessimism: Implications for theory, research, and practice.* (pp 189-216). Washington D.C.: American Psychological Association.

10. Snyder, C. R., & Lopez, S. J. (2007). *Positive psychology: The scientific and practical explorations of human strengths,* Thousand Oaks, CA: Sage Publications.

11. Evidence of the benefits of optimism, hope, and positive perspectives can be found in each of the books cited above. These benefits show

up in measures of health and longevity, as well as success at work, in schools, and in organizations where people work together for desired outcomes.

12. Fredrickson, B. L. (2003). "Positive emotions and upward spirals in organizations," In Cameron, K. S., Dutton, J. E., & Quinn, R. E. (Eds.) *Positive organizational scholarship: Foundations of a new discipline.* San Francisco: Berrett-Koehler Publishers. Similar results are reported in: Dutton, J. E. (2003). *Energize your workplace: How to create and sustain high-quality connections at work.* San Francisco: Jossey-Bass.

13. Clifton, D. O. & Harter, J. K. (2003). "Investing in strengths," In Cameron, K. S., Dutton, J. E., & Quinn, R. E. eds., *Positive organizational scholarship: Foundations of a new discipline.* San Francisco: Berrett-Koehler Publishers.

14. Fredrickson, B. L. & Losada, M. F. (2005). "Positive affect and the complex dynamics of human flourishing." *American Psychologist* 60: 678-86.

15. Gottman, J. M. (1994). *What predicts divorce? The relationship between marital processes and marital outcomes.* Hillsdale, NJ: Erlbaum.

16. Buckingham, M. & Clifton, D. O. (2001). *Now, discover your strengths.* NY: The Free Press.

17. Rath, T. (2007). *Strengths Finder 2.0,* New York City: Gallup Press.

18. Peterson, C. & Seligman, M. E. P. (2004). *Character strengths and virtues: A handbook and classification.* Washington D.C.: American Psychological Association.

19. Centre of Applied Positive Psychology. (2009). *Realise2.* Internet access address: <http://www.cappeu.org/realise2.htm>

PART 2:

HOW DO YOU FACILITATE THE *AST PROCESS?*

What are the guidelines for facilitating the process?

First, you will need to accept the responsibility of guiding others through the process. Fortunately, guiding others through this process is fairly easy. There is a packet for each participant, and each packet has explicit directions for carrying out the seven steps of the process. Despite the written directions in each packet, the initiation and implementation of the activities requires the overview and guidance of at least one person. That person will be called the *Guide*. The Guide facilitates the process and also is one of the four participants.

The person who has accepted the role of Guide can also share the role with another person. In this case, the two would get together and decide how they would share the responsibilities listed below.

The responsibilities of the Guide are:

(1) The Guide must understand the intended purpose and the general parameters of articulating strengths. Reading Part 1, the Guidelines in Part 2, and the Participant Packet, should enable you to attain this understanding. You are already well underway.

(2) The Guide should develop a general plan for implementing the process before inviting others to participate. A plan includes the place to meet, the day or days for meeting, and the materials needed for the process. There are four possible formats for completing the process. When the primary, or default, format is used, the AST process is completed in one session that takes about three hours. These guidelines are written with the assumption that the 3-hour, 1-meeting format will be used.

However, you may want to spread the process out by meeting two times, or three times, or without strict timing. If you want to consider these formats, read about alternative formats, which are described in section towards the end of PART 2.

(3) Since the AST is designed for four participants, the Guide must think of three other people who agree to try out this process. When inviting potential participants, the Guide needs to be very clear about the purposes of participating in the AST process, as well as the potential benefits of this process. Part I of this booklet provides ideas for describing purposes and benefits.

(4) After four participants have agreed, the time, the place, and the details of the format should be communicated to each. The setting for the gatherings should have privacy and sufficient space for the activities of the process. Ideally, the chairs should be movable, and there should be a small table or clipboards for writing support. The Guide should describe the costs and other obligations that are expected, such as: cost of the book and materials, rent for the meeting space, snacks, etc.).

(5) Before the first session, the Guide should obtain a timer that will allow rather precise timing of activities that take from 3 minutes up to 12 minutes during the Step 3 of the AST. <u>At least 3 pages of blank paper are needed in Step 3 for each participant.</u> Participants should be encouraged to bring along their own pad of paper and pencils or pens. After Step 3, each participant will need materials for making a poster, using felt-tipped pens of at least two colors. The Guide could bring the materials for making the poster, or ask each participant to bring his or her own. A light-colored file folder that has not been written upon works well for making a poster.

(6) The Guide should become very familiar with each of the activities and the steps of the process before the first session. The Participant Packets might be distributed to the participants before the first session, thereby increasing everyone's familiarity with the activities. Although distributing the packets to the potential participants is somewhat preferable, it is certainly not necessary. Four Participant Packets are included in the Appendices of this book. They should be cut out and

distributed to the four participants at the most appropriate time. If the Guide anticipates that there will be five participants, one photocopy of a packet can be made and used. If six or more participants are expected, two or more AST books should be purchased.

(7) Before the first scheduled session, the Guide should carefully study the Timing Worksheet shown on page 24, the last page before the Appendices. Note that if one of the alternative formats calling for two or three sessions is chosen, extra directions for facilitating these alternative formats can be located towards the back of Part 2. Also, a timing-worksheet for each of those alternative sessions can be located on pages 22 and 23. Each of these worksheets will provide an overview of all of the activities in that particular format of the process. Recommended times for each step are shown on the Timing Worksheet of the 3-hour, 1-session format. If one of the alternative formats is used, the Guide will need to write different times on each Participant Packet, before they are distributed.

(8) When all participants arrive for the first session of the AST process, the Guide should preview the session by focusing on the cover sheet for the Participant Packet. The four major activities of the AST process can be previewed first. The participants should be warned that the steps of the process will be timed, and that some of the activities may feel rushed. It might be agreed that the timing will be elongated if one or two participants have not completed a given section during the recommended time period. If timing is elongated, participants should be prepared to take more than three hours to complete the process. Participants should be told that a 10-minute break is scheduled after completion of Step 3, which is at the end of Activity #2, the Quad activity.

(9) The Guide should make sure that each participant has each of the following materials at the beginning of the 3-hour, 1-session format:

     o A Participant Packet
     o A pencil or pen
     o 3 blank sheets of paper
     o A blank, light-colored file folder
     o 2 felt-tipped pens of two different colors

What are the specific instructions for facilitating the 3-hour AST process?

If the Guide is using the standard continuous, three-hour session as the format for the AST process, he or she can follow the instructions suggested below:

(1)   Use no more than ten minutes to welcome participants and prepare them to start the formal part of the process, by making sure they know each other's names and that they have the necessary materials to start.

(2)   Set your timer for the Recommended Time listed after the Step number and title in your own Participant Packet. (It will be 15 minutes, for Step 1).

You can refer to the TIMING WORKSHEET FOR THE 3-HOUR AST PROCESS on page 24, for overall guidance, but you can set your timer at the appropriate time by just using the times shown in your own Participant Packet.

(3)   Continue to start each Step shown in the Participant Packet by setting your timer for the recommended time shown for each step. <u>Before you start the timer, make sure that each participant has had a chance to read the directions for the Step you are about to time</u>. Start the timing when all participants are ready to start the activities described by the instructions for doing the Step.

(4)   Provide a break of 10 minutes or more after completing Step 3 and before starting Step 4. This is right after the quad activity, where each participant has had 15 minutes each to talk about Good Experiences.

(5)   After the break, guide them through Steps 4, 5, and 6, wherein they work independently. When these steps are completed, everyone will have a poster showing four highly prioritized strengths, and they will be ready for the last interactive session, which is Step 7.

(6)   You then start Step 7 and participants present their posters to the group. After completing Step 7, you end the process by handing out the page in

the Appendices titled *A Post-AST Activity*. If there is time, you could have them read the page and discuss it before ending the AST process.

If you have decided to use one of the alternative formats, refer to specific instructions for each alternative format listed on pages 15 to 21.

Does the process work if you do not have exactly four people?

While this AST process was designed for use by quads, it can be modified if you only have three or if you should happen to have five.

If you have three people, you would have more time to complete Activity # 2, which includes Step 3, <u>Describing GE s and Identifying Possible Strengths</u>. However, in trios, each person only gets feedback from two other people, which lessens the impact of the experience. It is a trade off that may be necessary.

If you have five people, you need to expand the time of each small-group activity. This can be done, but you will need to lengthen the time spent in this interactive activity. If you have five participants using the 1-session format, you can complete it in three hours only if you follow strict timing guidelines.

If you have six people, you should probably split into two separate groups during the activities that require group interaction. This will save quite a bit of time because it reduces the group interaction time by half. If you do this, you should have two AST books.

What are the Alternative Formats for using the AST process?

The basic format for using the AST process is one that can be implemented in one three-hour session. This format is easiest to set up and it has the advantage of being completed before unforeseen complications arise, such as participants getting sick or canceling later sessions because of unexpected competing events at the time of second or third sessions. A possible disadvantage of doing all in one session is that participants might feel overwhelmed by the need to focus their attention for more than two hours at a time. There is little time for relaxed reflection when everything is done in one, three-hour session. Some participants feel that there are too many decisions to make and they get exhausted when they are faced with so many closely timed activities in a row.

To avoid the disadvantages of a three-hour, continuous session, you might consider one of the following alternative formats:

(1) Two separate sessions of 90 minutes each, with homework in between,
(2) Three 50-minute sessions, with homework between sessions.
(3) Untimed format, scheduled for one session or two sessions.

There are some advantages and some disadvantages of each format. Consider these advantages and disadvantages of each format:

Two 90-minute Sessions. This format may be the most satisfying way to complete the process if the participants can agree on the when-and-where of two scheduled sessions. The reason this format is less pressured is that much of the individualized work following the quad experience can be done at home, with unlimited time for analyzing and reflecting. This means that the two interactive sessions can be lengthened, leaving more time for feedback and discussion. Posters can be completed at home, where participants often have better materials and resources for making their posters.

(Additional instructions are available on the next few pages for facilitating two 90-minute sessions.)

Three 50-minute Sessions. This format works best if the participants are at a work setting or a school where sessions might be scheduled during the lunch hour or during 50-minute class sessions. It is also possible that participants could meet for fifty minutes after working hours, which would not be a big disruption to their daily schedules. This format also allows much of the homework to be done in the quiet of one's home, thereby leaving more time for interacting in the quad.

(Additional instructions for facilitating 3 fifty-minute sessions are provided later in this section)

Untimed Sessions. This format permits the most unpressured approach to the AST process. Participants can work at their own paces and the Guide does not need to use a timer. The Guide does not time the activities of the process, but instead keeps track of when each participant finishes each step of the process. When doing this, the Guide moves the group to the next step after the slowest participant has completed the current step.

This untimed format requires that a longer period of time be set aside to complete the whole process. If you are doing it in one session, four or even five hours might be set aside to complete it. If it is being done in two sessions, at least three hours should be set aside for the first session, and at least one hour should be set aside for the second session. Since much of the individual work is done between interactive sessions, this format works best for allowing people to work at their own pace.

Considering the variety of individual differences in most quads, two untimed sessions of three hours and one hour, provide the most relaxed and easily facilitated format for the AST process. The opportunity to have participants do much of their homework between sessions is a real advantage for allowing individuals to work at their own speed, rather than under the pressure of strict timing.

What are the specific instructions for facilitating two 90-minute sessions?

(1) Change the Recommended Times provided for each of the seven Steps of each Participant Packet located in the Appendices. To do that, cross out the number of minutes listed for each Step if it is different from the one listed, and replace the number with the following numbers:

Step 1: 20 minutes
Step 2: 10 minutes (no change)
Step 3: 15 minutes per person:(12 minutes describing GEs & 3 for feedback)
Step 4: Untimed, since it is done as homework between sessions.
Step 5: Untimed, since it is done as homework between sessions.
Step 6: Untimed, since it is done as homework between sessions.
Step 7: 90 minutes total, 20 minutes per person, plus 10 minutes wrap-up.

(Please refer to the Timing Worksheet on page 22 for an overview of the timing for the alternative format using two 90-minute sessions)

(2) When you start the session, use no more than ten minutes to welcome participants and prepare them to start the formal part of the process, by making sure they know the names of other participants. Also make sure that each has the materials they need for the session you are starting.

(3) Tell the participants that you will be timing the Steps listed in their Participant Packet. You can use the Recommended Times in your own Participant Packet for setting your timer.

Please note that <u>the timing starts after the participants have had time to read the instructions</u> for the Step being done next. This is particularly important before starting *Step 3: Describing GEs and Identifying Possible Strengths*, because these are complicated instructions. It usually takes about five minutes to read and understand instructions for Step 3.

(4) At the end of Session #1, remind participants that Steps 4, 5, & 6 need to be completed as homework before the next session. You can ask them to get their own materials for the poster they are to bring to the next session, or you can assemble and give to them the materials they will need. It is probably wise for you to give them each a light colored folder along with the Participant Packet. They can use this folder to keep their Participant Packet, until they use the file folder for their poster, called for in Step 6.

(5) When they reassemble for the second 90-minute session, tell them that they will have no more than fifteen minutes per person to show their poster and elaborate by describing the strengths and some of the events supporting the strengths. When all have had their time talking about their strengths, pass out the page in the Appendices titled *A Post-AST Activity*. Have a short discussion of this activity after they have read about it.

What are the specific instructions for facilitating three 50-minute sessions?

(1) Change the Recommended Times provided for each of the seven Steps of each Participant Packet in the Appendices. To do that, cross out the number of minutes listed for each Step if it is different from the one listed, and replace the number with the following numbers:

Step 1: 20 minutes
Step 2: 10 minutes (no change)
Step 3: 12 minutes per person: (10 minutes describing GEs & 2 for feedback)
   (See Guideline #2 below, to consider using trios rather than quads;
   If Trios are used, each person gets 13 minutes for GEs & 3 for feedback)
Step 4: Untimed, since it is done as homework between sessions.
Step 5: Untimed, since it is done as homework between sessions.

Step 6: Untimed, since it is done as homework between sessions.
Step 7: 50 minutes total, 10 minutes per person, plus 10 minutes wrap-up.

(Please refer to the Timing Worksheet on page 23 for an overview of the timing for the alternative format showing three 50-minute sessions.)

(2) Before the first session, try to determine if there will be at least 6 participants. If there are exactly three or six, use trios rather than quads. If there are five participants, try to schedule a fourth session and use two sessions for Step 3. If there are four participants, use quads.

(3) At the beginning of the first session, take around five minutes to describe what will happen in the three sessions, and mention that there will be homework between sessions that must be completed before the next session starts.

(4) Set your timer so that the Recommended Time listed after the next Step title, can be timed. Tell the participants that you will be timing the Steps listed in their Participant Packet. You can use the Recommended Times in your own Participant Packet for setting your timer.

Please note that <u>the timing starts after the participants have had time to read the instructions</u> for the Step being done next. This is particularly important before starting *Step 3: Describing GEs and Identifying Possible Strengths*, because these are complicated instructions. Luckily, in this 3-session format, the participants can read the instructions for Step 3 before they come to the next session. Remind them that they should have read the instructions for Step 3 as the primary homework for Session 2. They should also spend more time prior to session #2 on what they came up with during the first session when they did Steps 1 and 2.

(5) During Session #2 they will be doing Step 3. If in quads, they will have only twelve minutes for each participant. If in trios, they will have 16 minutes for each participant, 13 describing GEs and 3 for getting feedback.

(6) At the end of Session #2, remind participants that Steps 4, 5, & 6 need to be completed as homework before the next session. You can ask them

to get their own materials for the poster they are to make before the next session, or you can assemble and give to them the materials they will need. It is probably wise for you to give them each a light colored folder along with the Participant Packet. They can use this folder to carry their Participant Packet, and they can also use the folder for making their poster.

(7)   When they reassemble for the third 50-minute session, you tell them that they will have no more than 10 minutes per person to show their poster and elaborate by describing the strengths and some of the events supporting the strengths. If you arranged to have trios, they will each have 13 minutes for this. When all have had their time talking about their strengths, pass out the page in the Appendices titled *A Post-AST Activity*. Have a short discussion of this activity after they have read about it.

What are specific instructions for facilitating untimed sessions?

(1)   Decide if you want to complete the AST process in one session or two sessions. If you decide to do it in one session, you will probably ask participants to set aside five hours. If you decide to do the AST process in two sessions, you could set aside three hours for the first session and one hour for the second session. Participants would have about 90 minutes of homework between the two sessions.

(2)   Since you will not be timing the 7 Steps, start the session by explaining that people can work at their own speed when doing Steps 1 and 2. You need to keep track of the general progress of each participant, but you are really most attentive to the person who is the slowest completing Steps 1 and 2, because Step 3 cannot be started until all participants are done with Steps 1 and 2. The most difficult facilitation task is what you suggest to the participants who have completed Steps 1 and 2, and are waiting for the slowest participant to do the same. You might suggest that all participants go back and spend more time on Steps 1 and 2, since those activities can always be taken to deeper levels of exploration.

(3)   After all participants are ready start the interactive group process of Step 3, the Guide might suggest that everyone have about 15 minutes during which at least three Good Experiences are described and feedback about possible strengths is given. Since you are not actually

using a timer, this target figure of 15 minutes a person is not strictly enforced, but it does keep one or two people from going into too much detail, which could last for hours if left unchecked.

(4) If everyone has agreed that there will be a second session for presenting their posters to each other, the Guide would assign everyone the responsibility to complete Steps 4, 5, and 6 before returning for the second session. Settle on the exact time and place for the second session and end the first session.

(5) If you are doing all seven steps in one session, you might take a break after finishing Step 3, the quad experience. When everyone returns after the break, start everyone on Steps 4, 5, and 6, working at their own speed. As you did during Steps 1 and 2, you need to keep track of the slowest person to complete each step, and tell the faster people that they might go back and explore each step in more depth, because Step 7 can not be started until all participants are done with Steps 4, 5, and 6.

(6) When all participants have finished Step 6, the creation of a poster, you assemble as a group and encourage each to present his or her poster to others. Encourage participants to give reactions and suggestions for making posters clearer and/or more thoroughly elaborated.

If you are facilitating a group that had divided the AST process into two sessions, you follow the same process as mentioned above in the (6) instruction guideline.

(7) When the posters have been shared and discussed, move to the last activity, which is the distribution of the page in the Appendices titled: *A Post-AST Activity*. Have a short discussion of this activity after they have read about it, and end the AST process.

TIMING WORKSHEET FOR AN ALTERNATE FORMAT: Two 90-minute Sessions

Example	Start Time	Your Times	Instructions
6:00 PM	00:00 +(15)	_____	<u>Start the first of two 90-minute sessions.</u> Do Step 1: Identifying 4 GE s (individual time)
6:15	00:15 +(10)	_____	Do Step 2: Considering 107 examples of Strengths (individual time)
6:25	00:25 +(05)	_____	Guide asks participants to read page 4, How to do Step 3 Guide asks if they have questions before starting Step 3
6:30 6:30 6:45 7:00 7:15	00:30 +(60) 15" each if quad	_____ _____ _____	Start Step 3 (Group Time) <u>If Quad</u> <u>If Trio</u> 1st Talker (12+3 min.) 1st Talker (16+4 min.) 2nd Talker (12+3 min.) 2nd Talker(16+4 min.) 3rd Talker (12+3 min.) 3rd Talker(16+4 min.) 4th Talker (12+3 min.)
7:30	01:30	_____ _____	First 90" session is completed: Guide describes homework assignment of Steps 4, 5, and 6 be completed before next session.
Homework done at home		Work done at home	HOMEWORK ASSIGNMENT FOR NEXT 90" SESSION Do Step 4 (Organizing & Prioritizing – At least 15 min.) Do Step 5: Identifying actual events. (At least 15 min.) Do Step 6: Make a poster of Possible Dependable Strengths (At least 20 min.)
6:00 PM	00:00 +(90")	_____	<u>Start the second of the two 90-minute sessions.</u> Do Step 7: Presenting your Possible Strengths to others (Group time, 20 min. each for individual sharing)
7:30 PM	01:30	_____	Workbook process is completed: Plan follow-up Session

The activities required to implement this format takes two 90-minute sessions, plus homework. The activities should be directed by the Guide, who acts as a timer while guiding participants through the first 3 steps in accordance with the recommended times. The Guide can be one of the participants.

The Guide provides the 7-page packet to each participant, in addition to at least 3 blank pages for written feedback. The Guide may also distribute materials for making individualized posters, or ask each participant to obtain own materials. These poster materials can be light colored file folders accompanied with two felt-tipped pens of different color. Participants prepare for the second session by doing Steps 4-6 at home. If 5 participants are involved, the allotted times for group activities should be expanded appropriately. If there are 6, form two trios.

TIMING WORKSHEET for AN ALTERNATE FORMAT: Three 50-minute Sessions

Example	Start Time	Your Times	Instructions
12:00 noon	00:00 +(05)	_____	<u>Start the first of three 50-minute sessions.</u> Discuss what will happen in 3 sessions and in between.
12:05	00:05 +(20)	_____	Do Step 1: Identifying 4 GE s (20 min. individual time)
12:25	00:25 +(12)	_____	Each person shares one GE (group activity – 3 minutes per person sharing)
12:37	00:37 (+10)	_____	Start Step 2: Considering 107 examples of Strengths (10 min. individual time)
12:47	00:47 (+3)	_____	Discuss reactions to Step 2, and homework assignment of reading page 4, and being ready to do Step 3 at next mtg.
_____	_____	_____	<u>Start the second of three 50-minute sessions.</u>
12.00 PM	+(50)		Start Step 3 (50 min. Group Time) <u>If Quad</u> <u>If Trio</u>
12:00 12:12 12:24 12:36	12" each if quad	_____ _____ _____ _____	1st Talker (10+2 min.) 1st Talker (13+3 min.) 2nd Talker (10+2 min.) 2nd Talker(13+3 min.) 3rd Talker (10+2 min.) 3rd Talker(13+3 min.) 4th Talker (10+2 min.)
0:48	0:48 (+2)	_____	Second 50" session is completed: Guide describes homework assignment of Steps 4, 5, and 6 be completed before next session.
Done at home		Done at home	HOMEWORK ASSIGNMENT FOR NEXT 60" SESSION Do Step 4 (Organizing & Prioritizing – At least 15 min.) Do Step 5: Identifying actual events. (At least 15 min.) Do Step 6: Make a poster of Possible Dependable Strengths (At least 20 min.)
12:00 PM	00:00 +(48)	_____	<u>Start the third of the three 50-minute sessions.</u> Do Step 7: Presenting your Possible Strengths to others (Group time, 12 min. each for individual sharing)
0:48 PM	0:48 (+02)	_____	Workbook process is completed: Plan follow-up Session

The timing for the activities required to implement the format of three 50-minute sessions is shown above. Homework is required between sessions.

TIMING WORKSHEET FOR THE 3-HOUR AST PROCESS: The Primary Format Used

Example	Start Time	Your Times	Instructions
6:00 PM	00:00 +(15)	_____	<u>Ready to start</u> Do Step 1: Identifying 4 GE s (individual time)
6:15	00:15 +(10)	_____	Do Step 2: Considering 107 examples of Strengths (individual time)
6:25	00:25 +(05)	_____	Guide asks participants to read page 4, How to do Step 3 Guide asks if they have questions before starting Step 3
6:30	00:30 +(60)		Start Step 3 (Group Time)
6:30 6:45 7:00 7:15	15" each if quad	_____ _____ _____ _____	<u>If Quad</u> 1st Talker (12+3 min.) 2nd Talker (12+3 min.) 3rd Talker (12+3 min.) 4th Talker (12+3 min.) <u>If Trio</u> 1st Talker (16+4 min.) 2nd Talker (16+4 min.) 3rd Talker (16+4 min.)
7:30	01:30 +(10)	_____	Take 10 minute break
7:40	01:40 +(12)	_____	Do Step 4 (Organizing & Prioritizing – 12 min. indiv. time.)
7:52	01:52 +(12)	_____	Do Step 5: Identifying actual events. (12 minutes – indiv.)
8:04	02:04 +(16)	_____	Do Step 6: Make a poster of Possible Dependable Strengths (16 minutes of individual time)
8:20	02:20 +(20)	_____	Do Step 7: Presenting your Possible Strengths to others (Group time, 5 min. each for individual sharing)
8:40	02:40	_____	Workshop is completed: Plan follow-up Session

The activities required to implement this AST process takes nearly three hours. The activities should be directed by the Guide, who acts as a timer while guiding participants through the seven steps in accordance with the recommended times. The Guide can be one of the participants.

COVER PAGE FOR APPENDICES

APPENDIX I: Four copies of the 7-page <u>Participant Packet</u> for Articulating Strengths Together (AST)

APPENDIX II: Four copies of a Post-AST Activity: Creating Strength-Focused Relationships

Note: The materials in the Appendices were designed to be cut out* and distributed to the four individuals participating in the process of:

ARTICULATING STRENGTHS TOGETHER (AST): AN INTERACTIVE PROCESS TO ENHANCE POSITIVITY

* a razor blade, or some other sharp cutting instrument is recommended for removing these pages from the Appendices.

<u>**Participant Packet**</u>
for Articulating Strengths Together (AST)

This packet is organized into four major activities:
1) Preparing for the Quad activity
2) Participating in the Quad activity
3) Preparing for the Poster activity
4) Participating in the Poster activity

Activity # 1 includes <u>Step 1</u>, *Identifying four Good Experiences (GE s)* and <u>Step 2</u>, *Considering 107 examples of Possible Strengths.*

Activity # 2 includes <u>Step 3</u>, *Describing GE s and Identifying Possible Strengths.*

Activity # 3 includes <u>Step 4</u>, *Organizing and prioritizing your Strengths*; <u>Step 5</u>, Identifying *actual events when you demonstrated each Strength*, followed by a <u>Worksheet</u> for demonstrating Strengths; and <u>Step 6</u>, *Making a poster of your Strengths, with events that demonstrate each strength.*

Activity # 4 includes <u>Step 7</u>, *Presenting your Strengths to others.*

- -

This Participant Packet is found in the Appendices of the book:

Articulating Strengths Together (AST):
An Interactive Process to Enhance Positivity

Jerald R. Forster, PhD.
Center for Dependable Strengths

Step 1: Identifying four Good Experiences (GE s)
(Recommended Time: 15 minutes)

The definition of a <u>Good Experience</u> is:
> SOMETHING YOU FEEL YOU DID WELL,
> ENJOYED DOING, &
> ARE PROUD OF.

Elaborations:
- SOMETHING YOU <u>DID</u> …means you actively made it happen.
- <u>YOU</u> FEEL YOU DID WELL …it is your feeling that is important.
- All three criteria should apply to each Good Experience.
- Good Experiences (GE s) can come from <u>any time</u> or <u>any place</u> in your life's journey. Review your whole life for possibilities.
- A GE should be a specific, concrete event that describes a particular short story of your life. It has a beginning and an ending.
- A GE is often a small "triumph" in your life that gives you a sense of satisfaction and fulfillment.

Good Experience #1:

Good Experience #2:

Good Experience #3:

Good Experience #4:

Step 2: Considering 107 examples of Possible Strengths
(Recommended Time: 10 minutes)

This list of Possible Strengths is offered to suggest some words or phrases that can be used to describe strengths. There are only 107 examples on this list. There are many different words and phrases to describe strengths. These are offered to stimulate your thinking about different ways that your strengths might be described. Hopefully, before you identify four strengths to describe yourself for Step 7, you will think of even better words and phrases to describe your strengths.

To become more familiar with the words on this list, please read each word or phrase and underline the ones that might be appropriate for describing you. When you are finished circling those words, go back to those that were circled and underline four to six that might be the most appropriate for describing yourself.

107 examples of possible strengths:

Athletic, Resourceful, Adaptable, Motivated to Achieve, Organized, Initiator, Analytical, Managing, Altruistic, Playful, Ethical, Leader, Communicator, Competitive, Caring, Considerate, Broad perspective, Brave, Observant, Hopeful, Careful, Imaginative, Practical, Sensitive, Mentoring, Strong faith, Organized, Appreciative of beauty, Persistent, Disciplined, Authentic, Empathic, Evenhanded, Focused, Goal-Oriented, Curiosity, Socially responsible, Thinks ahead, Articulate, Cooperative, Tolerant, Creative, Kind, Grateful, Trustworthy, Aware of feelings, Honest, Artistic, Sees patterns, Brings people together, Sympathetic, Hospitable, Inquisitive, Cheerful, Intellectual, Self-controlled, Introspective, Follows through, Intelligent, Zestful, Lifetime learner, Inventive, Thrifty, Researching, Charismatic, Efficient, Fair, Open minded, Optimistic, Responsible, Problem solver, Intuitive, Self-confident, Intense, Friendly, Wisdom, Enthusiastic, Balanced, Prudent, Energetic, Generous, Responsible, Even tempered, Enjoys people, Witty, Courageous, Original, Diplomatic, Loyal, Skilled negotiator, Mechanical, Persuasive, Planner, Coordinating, Foresight, Critical thinker, Humility, Spiritual, Musical, Technical, Spatial, Computing.

Step 3: Describing GE s and Identifying Possible Strengths

(Recommended Time: 15 minutes per person;
12 min. describing GEs & 3 min. getting feedback)

What to do when in the quad:

(1)   In a quad, each participant will have around 12 minutes to describe 3 Good Experiences (GE s).

(2)   The others, who are in the group will listen and identify qualities they consider to be strengths the talker demonstrated during each GE. The listeners will list these strengths on a blank sheet of paper, which could be titled: Possible Strengths List. Later each listener will give the page of Possible Strengths to each talker after reading the list to the talker. Each page listing possible strengths should have the name of the talker at the top of the page.

(3)   When the first talker finishes talking about 3 GE s, the timer should check the time. If all three GE s were described in around 10 minutes, there will be time to describe the 4th GE. After about 12 minutes of talking time, the focus shifts to feedback. During the last three minutes of each talker's time, the other group members will tell the talker the strengths they noticed. After the oral feedback, each group person gives to the talker the written page of strengths prepared by the feedback person while the talker was talking.

(4)   After the first talker has gotten feedback, the attention shifts to the 2nd talker for about 15 minutes. After that the 3rd talker becomes the focus for about 15 minutes. After that, the 4th talker gets a turn.

Considerations if the small group is a trio or larger than a quad.

A.   Because a trio has only 3 participants, each participant will have around 20 minutes, instead of 15 minutes, to describe 3 GE s. This will usually mean that a fourth GE can be described.

B.   There is time for at least 2 minutes of feedback from both of the two listeners, meaning that each trio member has 16 minutes for talking about Good Experiences.

C.   If there are more than 4 participants, each talker adds 15 minutes to the total time required to complete this step, which adds up to more than 1 hour.

Step 4: Organizing and prioritizing your strengths
(Recommended Time: 12 minutes)

- Study the sheets of possible strengths you received from the other participants in your small group.
- Circle the ones that seem to be the best descriptions of your strengths and then add some of your own strengths-words that may not have been mentioned.
- Re-read through the 107 titles of possible strengths shown in Step 2 and <u>double-underline</u> those that you now claim as descriptors.
- From all of these lists of possible strengths, choose 7 to 9 strengths-words or phrases that best capture your own ideas of your strengths. List them below:

(1)
(2)
(3)
(4)
(5)
(6)
(7)
(8)
(9)

- After studying the list of 7-9 Strengths, choose the four strengths that seem to be your most valued and your most dependable. When choosing the four valued strengths, use the following criteria to evaluate each strength:

  ✓ Does this strength show up in many of my Good Experiences?
  ✓ Is the strength one that I have used often in the past?
  ✓ Is it a strength that I enjoy?
  ✓ Is it a strength that I strongly want in my future life?
  ✓ Am I *inner-motivated* to use the strength?

Then prioritize the four, listing the one you value the most first. List the four on the Worksheet shown below in Step 5.

Step 5: Identifying actual events when you demonstrated each strength.

(Recommended Time: 12 minutes)

After you have identified four Strengths, written their titles on the worksheet shown below, identify at least two past events or activities where you demonstrated each of the strengths. In a way, you are offering proofs that you have those strengths. Some of these events may be Good Experiences that you identified in Step 1. Other events that meet most of the criteria of a Good Experience (GE) might be used as proofs of the other strengths listed on the worksheet. Use a couple of key words or a phrase to identify each event, so that you could remember the event and describe it to someone if you were asked to do so.

Worksheet for Demonstrating Strengths

Strength #1: _____

1st Event: _____

2nd Event: _____

Strength #2: _____

1st Event: _____

2nd Event: _____

Strength #3: _____

1st Event: _____

2nd Event: _____

Strength #4: _____

1st Event: _____

2nd Event: _____

Step 6: Make a Poster of your Strengths, with events that demonstrate each strength.

(Recommended Time: 16 minutes)

Using the information from the Worksheet you just completed, make a poster that shows your four possible strengths with your best examples of events where you demonstrated each of the strengths.

Title the poster, **Four Strengths of (your name)**
(Make the words legible for readers at least four feet away)

It is recommended that you use a light colored file folder to make this poster. If you have two felt-tipped pens of different color, or two crayons, you might show your possible strengths in one color and the event that demonstrates the strength in a second color.

Step 7: Presenting your Strengths to others

(Recommended Time: 5 minutes per person)

During this last step of these activities, you will have some time to share the strengths you have identified. Hopefully, you might even be able to improve your wording or description of one or more of your strengths during this time of sharing. You might even ask for suggestions as to how you could communicate the meaning of one or more of the strengths you have identified.

It is useful to think of these particular strengths as draft descriptions that you are in the process of improving. Even after you complete these sessions, you will benefit from continuing your efforts to identify and communicate your strengths. Articulating your strengths, especially your Dependable Strengths®, should probably be a life-long activity that will continue to lead to new insights and more elaborate ways of communicating your self-identity. Use your poster as a first draft that you continue to elaborate and improve. Show improved posters to other people who might help you develop new posters that are more clear and useful for communicating your significant strengths. Also, continue to document the evidence supporting the strengths that you have identified.

Participant Packet
for Articulating Strengths Together (AST)

This packet is organized into four major activities:
1) Preparing for the Quad activity
2) Participating in the Quad activity
3) Preparing for the Poster activity
4) Participating in the Poster activity

Activity # 1 includes Step 1, *Identifying four Good Experiences (GE s)* and Step 2, *Considering 107 examples of Possible Strengths.*

Activity # 2 includes Step 3, *Describing GE s and Identifying Possible Strengths.*

Activity # 3 includes Step 4, *Organizing and prioritizing your Strengths;* Step 5, Identifying *actual events when you demonstrated each Strength,* followed by a Worksheet for demonstrating Strengths; and Step 6, *Making a poster of your Strengths, with events that demonstrate each strength.*

Activity # 4 includes Step 7, *Presenting your Strengths to others.*

- -

This Participant Packet is found in the Appendices of the book:

Articulating Strengths Together (AST):
An Interactive Process to Enhance Positivity

Jerald R. Forster, PhD.
Center for Dependable Strengths

Step 1: Identifying four Good Experiences (GE s)

(Recommended Time: 15 minutes)

The definition of a <u>Good Experience</u> is:
> SOMETHING YOU FEEL YOU DID WELL,
> ENJOYED DOING, &
> ARE PROUD OF.

Elaborations:
- SOMETHING YOU <u>DID</u> …means you actively made it happen.
- <u>YOU</u> FEEL YOU DID WELL …it is your feeling that is important.
- All three criteria should apply to each Good Experience.
- Good Experiences (GE s) can come from <u>any time</u> or <u>any place</u> in your life's journey. Review your whole life for possibilities.
- A GE should be a specific, concrete event that describes a particular short story of your life. It has a beginning and an ending.
- A GE is often a small "triumph" in your life that gives you a sense of satisfaction and fulfillment.

Good Experience #1:

Good Experience #2:

Good Experience #3:

Good Experience #4:

Step 2: Considering 107 examples of Possible Strengths

(Recommended Time: 10 minutes)

This list of Possible Strengths is offered to suggest some words or phrases that can be used to describe strengths. There are only 107 examples on this list. There are many different words and phrases to describe strengths. These are offered to stimulate your thinking about different ways that your strengths might be described. Hopefully, before you identify four strengths to describe yourself for Step 7, you will think of even better words and phrases to describe your strengths.

To become more familiar with the words on this list, please read each word or phrase and <u>circle the ones</u> that might be appropriate for describing you. When you are finished circling those words, go back to those that were circled and <u>underline four to six</u> that might be the <u>most appropriate</u> for describing yourself.

107 examples of possible strengths:

Athletic, Resourceful, Adaptable, Motivated to Achieve, Organized, Initiator, Analytical, Managing, Altruistic, Playful, Ethical, Leader, Communicator, Competitive, Caring, Considerate, Broad perspective, Brave, Observant, Hopeful, Careful, Imaginative, Practical, Sensitive, Mentoring, Strong faith, Organized, Appreciative of beauty, Persistent, Disciplined, Authentic, Empathic, Evenhanded, Focused, Goal-Oriented, Curiosity, Socially responsible, Thinks ahead, Articulate, Cooperative, Tolerant, Creative, Kind, Grateful, Trustworthy, Aware of feelings, Honest, Artistic, Sees patterns, Brings people together, Sympathetic, Hospitable, Inquisitive, Cheerful, Intellectual, Self-controlled, Introspective, Follows through, Intelligent, Zestful, Lifetime learner, Inventive, Thrifty, Researching, Charismatic, Efficient, Fair, Open minded, Optimistic, Responsible, Problem solver, Intuitive, Self-confident, Intense, Friendly, Wisdom, Enthusiastic, Balanced, Prudent, Energetic, Generous, Responsible, Even tempered, Enjoys people, Witty, Courageous, Original, Diplomatic, Loyal, Skilled negotiator, Mechanical, Persuasive, Planner, Coordinating, Foresight, Critical thinker, Humility, Spiritual, Musical, Technical, Spatial, Computing.

Step 3: Describing GE s and Identifying Possible Strengths

(Recommended Time: 15 minutes per person;
12 min. describing GEs & 3 min. getting feedback)

What to do when in the quad:

(1) In a quad, each participant will have around 12 minutes to describe 3 Good Experiences (GE s).

(2) The others, who are in the group will listen and identify qualities they consider to be strengths the talker demonstrated during each GE. The listeners will list these strengths on a blank sheet of paper, which could be titled: Possible Strengths List. Later each listener will give the page of Possible Strengths to each talker after reading the list to the talker. Each page listing possible strengths should have the name of the talker at the top of the page.

(3) When the first talker finishes talking about 3 GE s, the timer should check the time. If all three GE s were described in around 10 minutes, there will be time to describe the 4th GE. After about 12 minutes of talking time, the focus shifts to feedback. During the last three minutes of each talker's time, the other group members will tell the talker the strengths they noticed. After the oral feedback, each group person gives to the talker the written page of strengths prepared by the feedback person while the talker was talking.

(4) After the first talker has gotten feedback, the attention shifts to the 2nd talker for about 15 minutes. After that the 3rd talker becomes the focus for about 15 minutes. After that, the 4th talker gets a turn.

Considerations if the small group is a trio or larger than a quad.

A. Because a trio has only 3 participants, each participant will have around 20 minutes, instead of 15 minutes, to describe 3 GE s. This will usually mean that a fourth GE can be described.

B. There is time for at least 2 minutes of feedback from both of the two listeners, meaning that each trio member has 16 minutes for talking about Good Experiences.

C. If there are more than 4 participants, each talker adds 15 minutes to the total time required to complete this step, which adds up to more than 1 hour.

4

Step 4: Organizing and prioritizing your strengths

(Recommended Time: 12 minutes)

- Study the sheets of possible strengths you received from the other participants in your small group.
- Circle the ones that seem to be the best descriptions of your strengths and then add some of your own strengths-words that may not have been mentioned.
- Re-read through the 107 titles of possible strengths shown in Step 2 and double-underline those that you now claim as descriptors.
- From all of these lists of possible strengths, choose 7 to 9 strengths-words or phrases that best capture your own ideas of your strengths. List them below:

(1)
(2)
(3)
(4)
(5)
(6)
(7)
(8)
(9)

- After studying the list of 7-9 Strengths, choose the four strengths that seem to be your most valued and your most dependable. When choosing the four valued strengths, use the following criteria to evaluate each strength:

  ✓ Does this strength show up in many of my Good Experiences?
  ✓ Is the strength one that I have used often in the past?
  ✓ Is it a strength that I enjoy?
  ✓ Is it a strength that I strongly want in my future life?
  ✓ Am I *inner-motivated* to use the strength?

Then prioritize the four, listing the one you value the most first. List the four on the Worksheet shown below in Step 5.

Step 5: Identifying actual events when you demonstrated each strength.

(Recommended Time: 12 minutes)

After you have identified four Strengths, written their titles on the worksheet shown below, identify at least two past events or activities where you demonstrated each of the strengths. In a way, you are offering proofs that you have those strengths. Some of these events may be Good Experiences that you identified in Step 1. Other events that meet most of the criteria of a Good Experience (GE) might be used as proofs of the other strengths listed on the worksheet. Use a couple of key words or a phrase to identify each event, so that you could remember the event and describe it to someone if you were asked to do so.

Worksheet for Demonstrating Strengths

Strength #1: _____

1st Event: _____

2nd Event: _____

Strength #2: _____

1st Event: _____

2nd Event: _____

Strength #3: _____

1st Event: _____

2nd Event: _____

Strength #4: _____

1st Event: _____

2nd Event: _____

Step 6: Make a Poster of your Strengths, with events that demonstrate each strength.

(Recommended Time: 16 minutes)

Using the information from the Worksheet you just completed, make a poster that shows your four possible strengths with your best examples of events where you demonstrated each of the strengths.

Title the poster, **Four Strengths of (your name)**
(Make the words legible for readers at least four feet away)

It is recommended that you use a light colored file folder to make this poster. If you have two felt-tipped pens of different color, or two crayons, you might show your possible strengths in one color and the event that demonstrates the strength in a second color.

Step 7: Presenting your Strengths to others

(Recommended Time: 5 minutes per person)

During this last step of these activities, you will have some time to share the strengths you have identified. Hopefully, you might even be able to improve your wording or description of one or more of your strengths during this time of sharing. You might even ask for suggestions as to how you could communicate the meaning of one or more of the strengths you have identified.

It is useful to think of these particular strengths as draft descriptions that you are in the process of improving. Even after you complete these sessions, you will benefit from continuing your efforts to identify and communicate your strengths. Articulating your strengths, especially your Dependable Strengths®, should probably be a life-long activity that will continue to lead to new insights and more elaborate ways of communicating your self-identity. Use your poster as a first draft that you continue to elaborate and improve. Show improved posters to other people who might help you develop new posters that are more clear and useful for communicating your significant strengths. Also, continue to document the evidence supporting the strengths that you have identified.

Participant Packet
for Articulating Strengths Together (AST)

This packet is organized into four major activities:
1) Preparing for the Quad activity
2) Participating in the Quad activity
3) Preparing for the Poster activity
4) Participating in the Poster activity

Activity # 1 includes <u>Step 1</u>, *Identifying four Good Experiences (GE s)* and <u>Step 2</u>, *Considering 107 examples of Possible Strengths.*

Activity # 2 includes <u>Step 3</u>, *Describing GE s and Identifying Possible Strengths.*

Activity # 3 includes <u>Step 4</u>, *Organizing and prioritizing your Strengths;* <u>Step 5</u>, *Identifying actual events when you demonstrated each Strength,* followed by a <u>Worksheet</u> for demonstrating Strengths; and <u>Step 6</u>, *Making a poster of your Strengths, with events that demonstrate each strength.*

Activity # 4 includes <u>Step 7</u>, *Presenting your Strengths to others.*

- -

This Participant Packet is found in the Appendices of the book:

Articulating Strengths Together (AST):
An Interactive Process to Enhance Positivity

Jerald R. Forster, PhD.
Center for Dependable Strengths

Step 1: Identifying four Good Experiences (GE s)

(Recommended Time: 15 minutes)

The definition of a <u>Good Experience</u> is:
> SOMETHING YOU FEEL YOU DID WELL,
> ENJOYED DOING, &
> ARE PROUD OF.

Elaborations:
* SOMETHING YOU <u>DID</u> …means you actively made it happen.
* <u>YOU</u> FEEL YOU DID WELL …it is your feeling that is important.
* All three criteria should apply to each Good Experience.
* Good Experiences (GE s) can come from <u>any time</u> or <u>any place</u> in your life's journey. Review your whole life for possibilities.
* A GE should be a specific, concrete event that describes a particular short story of your life. It has a beginning and an ending.
* A GE is often a small "triumph" in your life that gives you a sense of satisfaction and fulfillment.

Good Experience #1:

Good Experience #2:

Good Experience #3:

Good Experience #4:

Step 2: Considering 107 examples of Possible Strengths
(Recommended Time: 10 minutes)

This list of Possible Strengths is offered to suggest some words or phrases that can be used to describe strengths. There are only 107 examples on this list. There are many different words and phrases to describe strengths. These are offered to stimulate your thinking about different ways that your strengths might be described. Hopefully, before you identify four strengths to describe yourself for Step 7, you will think of even better words and phrases to describe your strengths.

To become more familiar with the words on this list, please read each word or phrase and circle the ones that might be appropriate for describing you. When you are finished circling those words, go back to those that were circled and underline four to six that might be the most appropriate for describing yourself.

107 examples of possible strengths:

Athletic, Resourceful, Adaptable, Motivated to Achieve, Organized, Initiator, Analytical, Managing, Altruistic, Playful, Ethical, Leader, Communicator, Competitive, Caring, Considerate, Broad perspective, Brave, Observant, Hopeful, Careful, Imaginative, Practical, Sensitive, Mentoring, Strong faith, Organized, Appreciative of beauty, Persistent, Disciplined, Authentic, Empathic, Evenhanded, Focused, Goal-Oriented, Curiosity, Socially responsible, Thinks ahead, Articulate, Cooperative, Tolerant, Creative, Kind, Grateful, Trustworthy, Aware of feelings, Honest, Artistic, Sees patterns, Brings people together, Sympathetic, Hospitable, Inquisitive, Cheerful, Intellectual, Self-controlled, Introspective, Follows through, Intelligent, Zestful, Lifetime learner, Inventive, Thrifty, Researching, Charismatic, Efficient, Fair, Open minded, Optimistic, Responsible, Problem solver, Intuitive, Self-confident, Intense, Friendly, Wisdom, Enthusiastic, Balanced, Prudent, Energetic, Generous, Responsible, Even tempered, Enjoys people, Witty, Courageous, Original, Diplomatic, Loyal, Skilled negotiator, Mechanical, Persuasive, Planner, Coordinating, Foresight, Critical thinker, Humility, Spiritual, Musical, Technical, Spatial, Computing.

Step 3: Describing GE s and Identifying Possible Strengths

(Recommended Time: 15 minutes per person;
12 min. describing GEs & 3 min. getting feedback)

What to do when in the quad:

(1) In a quad, each participant will have around 12 minutes to describe 3 Good Experiences (GE s).

(2) The others, who are in the group will listen and identify qualities they consider to be strengths the talker demonstrated during each GE. The listeners will list these strengths on a blank sheet of paper, which could be titled: Possible Strengths List. Later each listener will give the page of Possible Strengths to each talker after reading the list to the talker. Each page listing possible strengths should have the name of the talker at the top of the page.

(3) When the first talker finishes talking about 3 GE s, the timer should check the time. If all three GE s were described in around 10 minutes, there will be time to describe the 4th GE. After about 12 minutes of talking time, the focus shifts to feedback. During the last three minutes of each talker's time, the other group members will tell the talker the strengths they noticed. After the oral feedback, each group person gives to the talker the written page of strengths prepared by the feedback person while the talker was talking.

(4) After the first talker has gotten feedback, the attention shifts to the 2nd talker for about 15 minutes. After that the 3rd talker becomes the focus for about 15 minutes. After that, the 4th talker gets a turn.

Considerations if the small group is a trio or larger than a quad.

A. Because a trio has only 3 participants, each participant will have around 20 minutes, instead of 15 minutes, to describe 3 GE s. This will usually mean that a fourth GE can be described.

B. There is time for at least 2 minutes of feedback from both of the two listeners, meaning that each trio member has 16 minutes for talking about Good Experiences.

C. If there are more than 4 participants, each talker adds 15 minutes to the total time required to complete this step, which adds up to more than 1 hour.

Step 4: Organizing and prioritizing your strengths

(Recommended Time: 12 minutes)

- Study the sheets of possible strengths you received from the other participants in your small group.
- Circle the ones that seem to be the best descriptions of your strengths and then add some of your own strengths-words that may not have been mentioned.
- Re-read through the 107 titles of possible strengths shown in Step 2 and double-underline those that you now claim as descriptors.
- From all of these lists of possible strengths, choose 7 to 9 strengths-words or phrases that best capture your own ideas of your strengths. List them below:

(1)
(2)
(3)
(4)
(5)
(6)
(7)
(8)
(9)

- After studying the list of 7-9 Strengths, choose the four strengths that seem to be your most valued and your most dependable. When choosing the four valued strengths, use the following criteria to evaluate each strength:

  ✓ Does this strength show up in many of my Good Experiences?
  ✓ Is the strength one that I have used often in the past?
  ✓ Is it a strength that I enjoy?
  ✓ Is it a strength that I strongly want in my future life?
  ✓ Am I *inner-motivated* to use the strength?

Then prioritize the four, listing the one you value the most first. List the four on the Worksheet shown below in Step 5.

Step 5: Identifying actual events when you demonstrated each strength.

(Recommended Time: 12 minutes)

After you have identified four Strengths, written their titles on the worksheet shown below, identify at least two past events or activities where you demonstrated each of the strengths. In a way, you are offering proofs that you have those strengths. Some of these events may be Good Experiences that you identified in Step 1. Other events that meet most of the criteria of a Good Experience (GE) might be used as proofs of the other strengths listed on the worksheet. Use a couple of key words or a phrase to identify each event, so that you could remember the event and describe it to someone if you were asked to do so.

Worksheet for Demonstrating Strengths

Strength #1: _____

1st Event: _____

2nd Event: _____

Strength #2: _____

1st Event: _____

2nd Event: _____

Strength #3: _____

1st Event: _____

2nd Event: _____

Strength #4: _____

1st Event: _____

2nd Event: _____

Step 6: Make a Poster of your Strengths, with events that demonstrate each strength.

(Recommended Time: 16 minutes)

Using the information from the Worksheet you just completed, make a poster that shows your four possible strengths with your best examples of events where you demonstrated each of the strengths.

Title the poster, **Four Strengths of (your name)**
(Make the words legible for readers at least four feet away)

It is recommended that you use a light colored file folder to make this poster. If you have two felt-tipped pens of different color, or two crayons, you might show your possible strengths in one color and the event that demonstrates the strength in a second color.

Step 7: Presenting your Strengths to others

(Recommended Time: 5 minutes per person)

During this last step of these activities, you will have some time to share the strengths you have identified. Hopefully, you might even be able to improve your wording or description of one or more of your strengths during this time of sharing. You might even ask for suggestions as to how you could communicate the meaning of one or more of the strengths you have identified.

It is useful to think of these particular strengths as draft descriptions that you are in the process of improving. Even after you complete these sessions, you will benefit from continuing your efforts to identify and communicate your strengths. Articulating your strengths, especially your Dependable Strengths®, should probably be a life-long activity that will continue to lead to new insights and more elaborate ways of communicating your self-identity. Use your poster as a first draft that you continue to elaborate and improve. Show improved posters to other people who might help you develop new posters that are more clear and useful for communicating your significant strengths. Also, continue to document the evidence supporting the strengths that you have identified.

Participant Packet
for Articulating Strengths Together (AST)

This packet is organized into four major activities:
1) Preparing for the Quad activity
2) Participating in the Quad activity
3) Preparing for the Poster activity
4) Participating in the Poster activity

Activity # 1 includes <u>Step 1</u>, *Identifying four Good Experiences (GE s)* and <u>Step 2</u>, *Considering 107 examples of Possible Strengths.*

Activity # 2 includes <u>Step 3</u>, *Describing GE s and Identifying Possible Strengths.*

Activity # 3 includes <u>Step 4</u>, *Organizing and prioritizing your Strengths;* <u>Step 5</u>, Identifying *actual events when you demonstrated each Strength,* followed by a <u>Worksheet</u> for demonstrating Strengths; and <u>Step 6</u>, *Making a poster of your Strengths,* with events *that demonstrate each strength.*

Activity # 4 includes <u>Step 7</u>, *Presenting your Strengths to others.*

- -

This Participant Packet is found in the Appendices of the book:

Articulating Strengths Together (AST):
An Interactive Process to Enhance Positivity

Jerald R. Forster, PhD.
Center for Dependable Strengths

Step 1: Identifying four Good Experiences (GE s)

The definition of a <u>Good Experience</u> is:
>   SOMETHING YOU FEEL YOU DID WELL,
>   ENJOYED DOING, &
>   ARE PROUD OF.

Elaborations:
*   SOMETHING YOU <u>DID</u> …means you actively made it happen.
*   <u>YOU</u> FEEL YOU DID WELL …it is your feeling that is important.
*   All three criteria should apply to each Good Experience.
*   Good Experiences (GE s) can come from <u>any time</u> or <u>any place</u> in your life's journey. Review your whole life for possibilities.
*   A GE should be a specific, concrete event that describes a particular short story of your life. It has a beginning and an ending.
*   A GE is often a small "triumph" in your life that gives you a sense of satisfaction and fulfillment.

Good Experience #1:

Good Experience #2:

Good Experience #3:

Good Experience #4:

Step 2: Considering 107 examples of Possible Strengths

(Recommended Time: 10 minutes)

This list of Possible Strengths is offered to suggest some words or phrases that can be used to describe strengths. There are only 107 examples on this list. There are many different words and phrases to describe strengths. These are offered to stimulate your thinking about different ways that your strengths might be described. Hopefully, before you identify four strengths to describe yourself for Step 7, you will think of even better words and phrases to describe your strengths.

To become more familiar with the words on this list, please read each word or phrase and <u>circle the ones</u> that might be appropriate for describing you. When you are finished circling those words, go back to those that were circled and <u>underline four to six</u> that might be the <u>most appropriate</u> for describing yourself.

107 examples of possible strengths:

Athletic, Resourceful, Adaptable, Motivated to Achieve, Organized, Initiator, Analytical, Managing, Altruistic, Playful, Ethical, Leader, Communicator, Competitive, Caring, Considerate, Broad perspective, Brave, Observant, Hopeful, Careful, Imaginative, Practical, Sensitive, Mentoring, Strong faith, Organized, Appreciative of beauty, Persistent, Disciplined, Authentic, Empathic, Evenhanded, Focused, Goal-Oriented, Curiosity, Socially responsible, Thinks ahead, Articulate, Cooperative, Tolerant, Creative, Kind, Grateful, Trustworthy, Aware of feelings, Honest, Artistic, Sees patterns, Brings people together, Sympathetic, Hospitable, Inquisitive, Cheerful, Intellectual, Self-controlled, Introspective, Follows through, Intelligent, Zestful, Lifetime learner, Inventive, Thrifty, Researching, Charismatic, Efficient, Fair, Open minded, Optimistic, Responsible, Problem solver, Intuitive, Self-confident, Intense, Friendly, Wisdom, Enthusiastic, Balanced, Prudent, Energetic, Generous, Responsible, Even tempered, Enjoys people, Witty, Courageous, Original, Diplomatic, Loyal, Skilled negotiator, Mechanical, Persuasive, Planner, Coordinating, Foresight, Critical thinker, Humility, Spiritual, Musical, Technical, Spatial, Computing.

Step 3: Describing GE s and Identifying Possible Strengths

(Recommended Time: 15 minutes per person;
12 min. describing GEs & 3 min. getting feedback)

What to do when in the quad:

(1) In a quad, each participant will have around 12 minutes to describe 3 Good Experiences (GE s).

(2) The others, who are in the group will listen and identify qualities they consider to be strengths the talker demonstrated during each GE. The listeners will list these strengths on a blank sheet of paper, which could be titled: Possible Strengths List. Later each listener will give the page of Possible Strengths to each talker after reading the list to the talker. Each page listing possible strengths should have the name of the talker at the top of the page.

(3) When the first talker finishes talking about 3 GE s, the timer should check the time. If all three GE s were described in around 10 minutes, there will be time to describe the 4th GE. After about 12 minutes of talking time, the focus shifts to feedback. During the last three minutes of each talker's time, the other group members will tell the talker the strengths they noticed. After the oral feedback, each group person gives to the talker the written page of strengths prepared by the feedback person while the talker was talking.

(4) After the first talker has gotten feedback, the attention shifts to the 2nd talker for about 15 minutes. After that the 3rd talker becomes the focus for about 15 minutes. After that, the 4th talker gets a turn.

Considerations if the small group is a trio or larger than a quad.

A. Because a trio has only 3 participants, each participant will have around 20 minutes, instead of 15 minutes, to describe 3 GE s. This will usually mean that a fourth GE can be described.

B. There is time for at least 2 minutes of feedback from both of the two listeners, meaning that each trio member has 16 minutes for talking about Good Experiences.

C. If there are more than 4 participants, each talker adds 15 minutes to the total time required to complete this step, which adds up to more than 1 hour.

Step 4: Organizing and prioritizing your strengths
(Recommended Time: 12 minutes)

- Study the sheets of possible strengths you received from the other participants in your small group.
- Circle the ones that seem to be the best descriptions of your strengths and then add some of your own strengths-words that may not have been mentioned.
- Re-read through the 107 titles of possible strengths shown in Step 2 and <u>double-underline</u> those that you now claim as descriptors.
- From all of these lists of possible strengths, choose 7 to 9 strengths-words or phrases that best capture your own ideas of your strengths. List them below:

(1)
(2)
(3)
(4)
(5)
(6)
(7)
(8)
(9)

- After studying the list of 7-9 Strengths, choose the four strengths that seem to be your most valued and your most dependable. When choosing the four valued strengths, use the following criteria to evaluate each strength:

  ✓ Does this strength show up in many of my Good Experiences?
  ✓ Is the strength one that I have used often in the past?
  ✓ Is it a strength that I enjoy?
  ✓ Is it a strength that I strongly want in my future life?
  ✓ Am I *inner-motivated* to use the strength?

Then prioritize the four, listing the one you value the most first. List the four on the Worksheet shown below in Step 5.

Step 5: Identifying actual events when you demonstrated each strength.

(Recommended Time: 12 minutes)

After you have identified four Strengths, written their titles on the worksheet shown below, identify at least two past events or activities where you demonstrated each of the strengths. In a way, you are offering proofs that you have those strengths. Some of these events may be Good Experiences that you identified in Step 1. Other events that meet most of the criteria of a Good Experience (GE) might be used as proofs of the other strengths listed on the worksheet. Use a couple of key words or a phrase to identify each event, so that you could remember the event and describe it to someone if you were asked to do so.

Worksheet for Demonstrating Strengths

Strength #1: _____

1st Event: _____

2nd Event: _____

Strength #2: _____

1st Event: _____

2nd Event: _____

Strength #3: _____

1st Event: _____

2nd Event: _____

Strength #4: _____

1st Event: _____

2nd Event: _____

Step 6: Make a Poster of your Strengths, with events that demonstrate each strength.

(Recommended Time: 16 minutes)

Using the information from the Worksheet you just completed, make a poster that shows your four possible strengths with your best examples of events where you demonstrated each of the strengths.

Title the poster, **Four Strengths of (your name)**
(Make the words legible for readers at least four feet away)

It is recommended that you use a light colored file folder to make this poster. If you have two felt-tipped pens of different color, or two crayons, you might show your possible strengths in one color and the event that demonstrates the strength in a second color.

Step 7: Presenting your Strengths to others

(Recommended Time: 5 minutes per person)

During this last step of these activities, you will have some time to share the strengths you have identified. Hopefully, you might even be able to improve your wording or description of one or more of your strengths during this time of sharing. You might even ask for suggestions as to how you could communicate the meaning of one or more of the strengths you have identified.

It is useful to think of these particular strengths as draft descriptions that you are in the process of improving. Even after you complete these sessions, you will benefit from continuing your efforts to identify and communicate your strengths. Articulating your strengths, especially your Dependable Strengths®, should probably be a life-long activity that will continue to lead to new insights and more elaborate ways of communicating your self-identity. Use your poster as a first draft that you continue to elaborate and improve. Show improved posters to other people who might help you develop new posters that are more clear and useful for communicating your significant strengths. Also, continue to document the evidence supporting the strengths that you have identified.

A POST-AST ACTIVITY:
CREATING STRENGTHS-FOCUSED RELATIONSHIPS

Introduction. You have just experienced an interactive process wherein you articulated your strengths with others. If you are like most participants in the AST process, you have become more aware of those experiences you remember with pride, enjoyment and engagement. You shared your good experiences with others and they helped you articulate themes for characterizing your significant and reliable strengths. You have organized and presented your strengths to others by creating a poster. Now it is time to use what you have experienced to increase the positivity of your relations with others. It is time to intentionally create more strengths-focused relationships in your life.

What is a Strengths-Focused Relationship? It is a relationship between two people who are aware of each other's strengths and who think of each other in terms of those strengths. To be aware of another's strengths, you need to know how the other person characterizes her/himself in terms of strengths. This means that each person in the relationship has articulated his/her strengths and shared them with the other. It also means that both people in the relationship have shared some of their best experiences and identified strengths that were used to make those experiences happen. We are talking about feelings of pride and enjoyment, two criteria used to identify Good Experiences.

This does not mean that you need to go through the formal AST process of identifying Good Experiences and articulating strengths. You just need to spend time together talking about good experiences each of you have had, as well as strengths you each *own*. To own an *articulated strength*, you have to feel that it does characterize you, and that, if you wanted to, you could talk about experiences where you demonstrated the strength. This does not mean that you brag about yourself. You just talk about yourself in terms of your best experiences and your best qualities. Each participant in the relationship agrees to do this as an intentional activity, because each wants to relate to each other in terms of strengths.

To intentionally establish a strengths-focused relationship does not mean that you always talk about positive experiences and strengths when relating to each other. It just means that you build a solid base of positive regard based on strengths, while also helping each other get through the troubles and trials of your lives. People in relationships that are strengths-based can deal with

problems better than those in relationships where one person feels he or she is helping out someone who is less able and/or more needy. Everyone has needs, problems, and negativity in their lives. Given this likelihood, these same individuals can deal with their issues most effectively with the help of people who know and acknowledge their strengths and their resiliency.

A POST-AST ACTIVITY:
CREATING STRENGTHS-FOCUSED RELATIONSHIPS

Introduction. You have just experienced an interactive process wherein you articulated your strengths with others. If you are like most participants in the AST process, you have become more aware of those experiences you remember with pride, enjoyment and engagement. You shared your good experiences with others and they helped you articulate themes for characterizing your significant and reliable strengths. You have organized and presented your strengths to others by creating a poster. Now it is time to use what you have experienced to increase the positivity of your relations with others. It is time to intentionally create more strengths-focused relationships in your life.

What is a Strengths-Focused Relationship? It is a relationship between two people who are aware of each other's strengths and who think of each other in terms of those strengths. To be aware of another's strengths, you need to know how the other person characterizes her/himself in terms of strengths. This means that each person in the relationship has articulated his/her strengths and shared them with the other. It also means that both people in the relationship have shared some of their best experiences and identified strengths that were used to make those experiences happen. We are talking about feelings of pride and enjoyment, two criteria used to identify Good Experiences.

This does not mean that you need to go through the formal AST process of identifying Good Experiences and articulating strengths. You just need to spend time together talking about good experiences each of you have had, as well as strengths you each *own*. To own an *articulated strength*, you have to feel that it does characterize you, and that, if you wanted to, you could talk about experiences where you demonstrated the strength. This does not mean that you brag about yourself. You just talk about yourself in terms of your best experiences and your best qualities. Each participant in the relationship agrees to do this as an intentional activity, because each wants to relate to each other in terms of strengths.

To intentionally establish a strengths-focused relationship does not mean that you always talk about positive experiences and strengths when relating to each other. It just means that you build a solid base of positive regard based on strengths, while also helping each other get through the troubles and trials of your lives. People in relationships that are strengths-based can deal with

problems better than those in relationships where one person feels he or she is helping out someone who is less able and/or more needy. Everyone has needs, problems, and negativity in their lives. Given this likelihood, these same individuals can deal with their issues most effectively with the help of people who know and acknowledge their strengths and their resiliency.

A POST-AST ACTIVITY:
CREATING STRENGTHS-FOCUSED RELATIONSHIPS

Introduction. You have just experienced an interactive process wherein you articulated your strengths with others. If you are like most participants in the AST process, you have become more aware of those experiences you remember with pride, enjoyment and engagement. You shared your good experiences with others and they helped you articulate themes for characterizing your significant and reliable strengths. You have organized and presented your strengths to others by creating a poster. Now it is time to use what you have experienced to increase the positivity of your relations with others. It is time to intentionally create more strengths-focused relationships in your life.

What is a Strengths-Focused Relationship? It is a relationship between two people who are aware of each other's strengths and who think of each other in terms of those strengths. To be aware of another's strengths, you need to know how the other person characterizes her/himself in terms of strengths. This means that each person in the relationship has articulated his/her strengths and shared them with the other. It also means that both people in the relationship have shared some of their best experiences and identified strengths that were used to make those experiences happen. We are talking about feelings of pride and enjoyment, two criteria used to identify Good Experiences.

This does not mean that you need to go through the formal AST process of identifying Good Experiences and articulating strengths. You just need to spend time together talking about good experiences each of you have had, as well as strengths you each *own*. To own an *articulated strength*, you have to feel that it does characterize you, and that, if you wanted to, you could talk about experiences where you demonstrated the strength. This does not mean that you brag about yourself. You just talk about yourself in terms of your best experiences and your best qualities. Each participant in the relationship agrees to do this as an intentional activity, because each wants to relate to each other in terms of strengths.

To intentionally establish a strengths-focused relationship does not mean that you always talk about positive experiences and strengths when relating to each other. It just means that you build a solid base of positive regard based on strengths, while also helping each other get through the troubles and trials of your lives. People in relationships that are strengths-based can deal with

problems better than those in relationships where one person feels he or she is helping out someone who is less able and/or more needy. Everyone has needs, problems, and negativity in their lives. Given this likelihood, these same individuals can deal with their issues most effectively with the help of people who know and acknowledge their strengths and their resiliency.

A POST-AST ACTIVITY:
CREATING STRENGTHS-FOCUSED RELATIONSHIPS

Introduction. You have just experienced an interactive process wherein you articulated your strengths with others. If you are like most participants in the AST process, you have become more aware of those experiences you remember with pride, enjoyment and engagement. You shared your good experiences with others and they helped you articulate themes for characterizing your significant and reliable strengths. You have organized and presented your strengths to others by creating a poster. Now it is time to use what you have experienced to increase the positivity of your relations with others. It is time to intentionally create more strengths-focused relationships in your life.

What is a Strengths-Focused Relationship? It is a relationship between two people who are aware of each other's strengths and who think of each other in terms of those strengths. To be aware of another's strengths, you need to know how the other person characterizes her/himself in terms of strengths. This means that each person in the relationship has articulated his/her strengths and shared them with the other. It also means that both people in the relationship have shared some of their best experiences and identified strengths that were used to make those experiences happen. We are talking about feelings of pride and enjoyment, two criteria used to identify Good Experiences.

This does not mean that you need to go through the formal AST process of identifying Good Experiences and articulating strengths. You just need to spend time together talking about good experiences each of you have had, as well as strengths you each *own*. To own an *articulated strength*, you have to feel that it does characterize you, and that, if you wanted to, you could talk about experiences where you demonstrated the strength. This does not mean that you brag about yourself. You just talk about yourself in terms of your best experiences and your best qualities. Each participant in the relationship agrees to do this as an intentional activity, because each wants to relate to each other in terms of strengths.

To intentionally establish a strengths-focused relationship does not mean that you always talk about positive experiences and strengths when relating to each other. It just means that you build a solid base of positive regard based on strengths, while also helping each other get through the troubles and trials of your lives. People in relationships that are strengths-based can deal with

problems better than those in relationships where one person feels he or she is helping out someone who is less able and/or more needy. Everyone has needs, problems, and negativity in their lives. Given this likelihood, these same individuals can deal with their issues most effectively with the help of people who know and acknowledge their strengths and their resiliency.

* * *

Made in the USA
Charleston, SC
21 January 2014